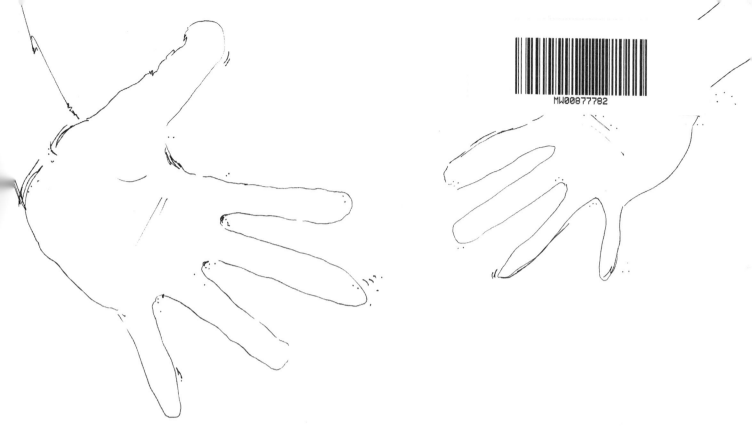

Don't Touch My Baby!

Written by Glenn Glazer
Illustrated by Ashleigh Walters

A Walk With Camden LLC
ISBN 978-1545144794

"This is dedicated to my family...
but mostly my son, who actually
had to put up with all of the
stuff in this book!!

G. Gasp

Don't Touch My Baby!

A Book for the Current, or Soon-to-Be, OCD Parent

The following pages are based on real events...

Hi stranger walking in the mall,
Person I don't know at all,
Thanks for holding my kid's hand,
So he can eat your viral strand!!

Oh weirdo strolling down the street,
Why are you touching my son's feet,
I know his socks seem real far south,
But he can put them in his mouth.

Ummm, server at the coffee shop,
With that bus pan full of slop,

You want to give my son pink eye?
You squeezed his cheek,
    while walking by!!

Yikes lady in the grocery aisle,
Eyes locked and that creepy smile,
Just 'cause you have kids at home,
You can't go kissing my kid's dome!

Yo old man, should I have said,
    "Way to sneeze on my son's head?"
        You lack a little style and grace,
            But your aim is good, you got his face!

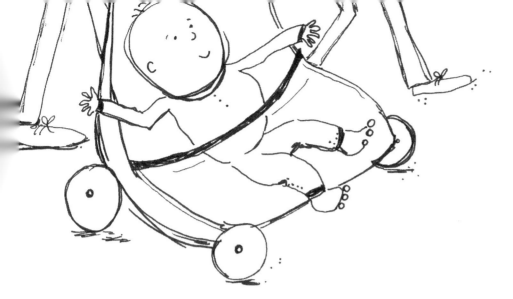

Nice old lady at the fair,
   With wise eyes and light gray hair,
      Don't put your finger on his nose
         And then pretend to eat his toes.

Trapped inside an elevator,
    Breathing like a respirator,
        Slimy dude looks like a frog,
            Don't pet my child like a dog.

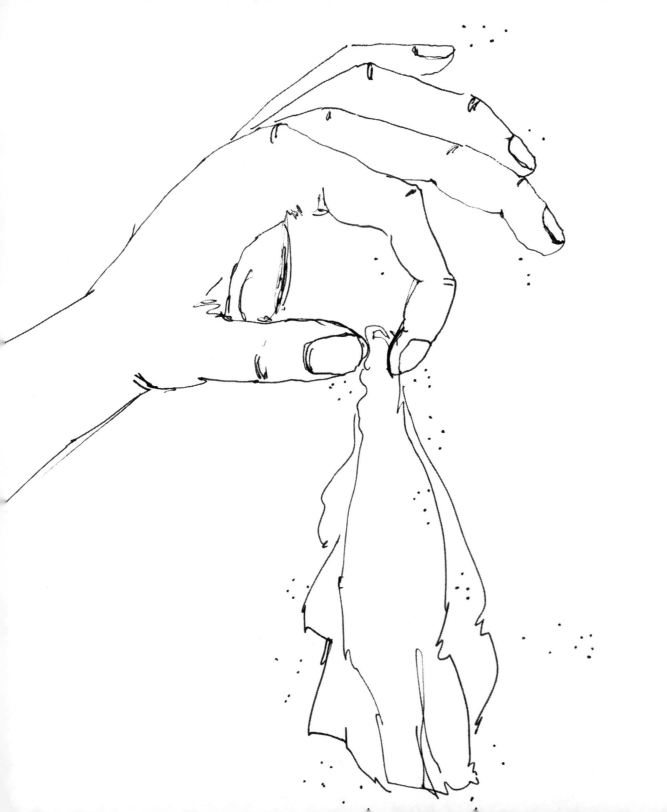

I don't mean to be a nag,
 Did ya hand my son a dirty rag?
  Here have it back, and please take off,
   While we enjoy your whooping cough.

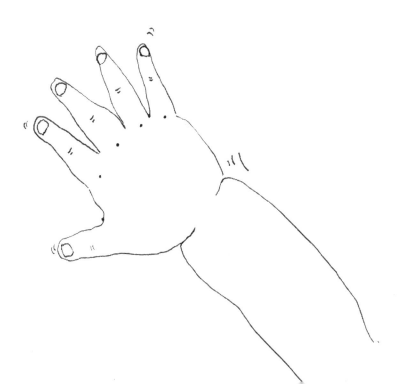

Girl are you from crazy town?
You'd better put your damn arms down,
Nothing you just said or did,
Convinced me you should hold my kid.

I don't care if you used gel,
And rubbed your hands
with wipes as well,

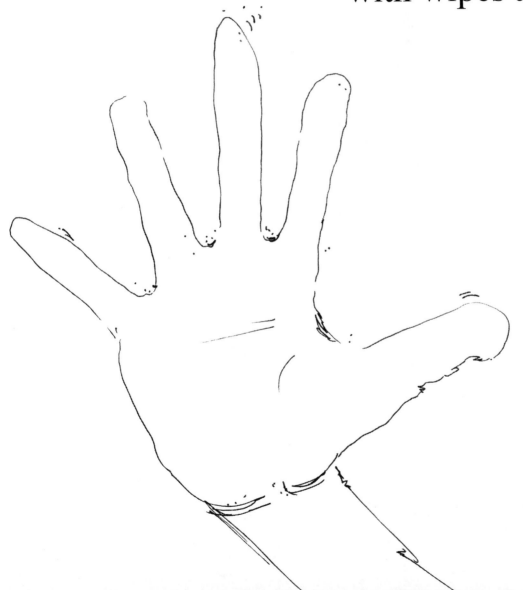

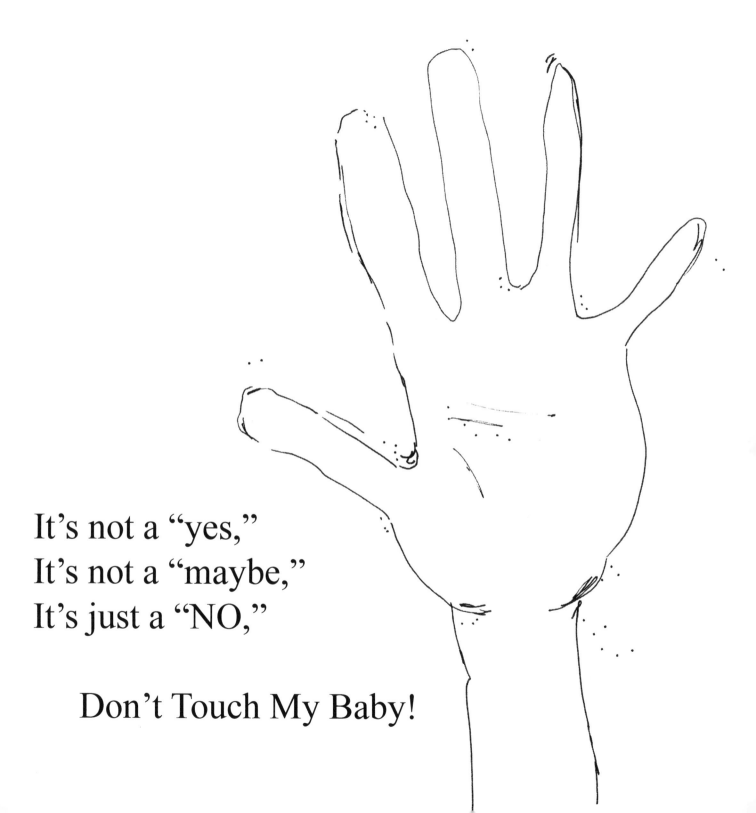

It's not a "yes,"
It's not a "maybe,"
It's just a "NO,"

Don't Touch My Baby!

About the Author and Illustrator

Glenn and Ashleigh met at work and quickly became very good friends. When Glenn discovered what an amazingly talented person Ashleigh is (outside of work), he and his wife commissioned her to paint an incredible mural in their son's nursery of Winnie the Pooh's Hundred Acre Woods.

Glenn then began talking to Ashleigh about the children's books he had written, and they decided to give it a go. It turned out to be a perfect collaboration.

Glenn and Ashleigh have another book in the works together, so look for that to be published in the near future.

Glenn Glazer is a television meteorologist, former talk show host, and the father of two hilarious little kids.

He has been writing poetry and short stories since he was a child, and has always been inspired by authors like Shel Silverstein and Dr. Seuss.

To date, Glenn has written many children's books, but this is the only book for adults he has written… and it's based on real events.

Glenn draws inspiration from his wife, his kids, and his dog (and best friend of 14 years) Camden, who passed away recently. (Note: His publishing company is called "A Walk with Camden")

Glenn is working with several artists on some of his other books, so look for those to be published very soon.

Ashleigh Walters is a television news anchor who earned degrees in both Journalism and Fine Arts Painting from the University of Colorado at Boulder.

Her paintings have been selected for exhibits at Palm Beach International Airport and CNN International, and her work has been animated into several television commercials.

Ashleigh uses acrylic, watercolor, ink, oil and photography. She shares her unique artistic perspective of the world

with news viewers on social media. View Ashleigh's art: www.ashleighwalters.net

Made in the USA
San Bernardino, CA
21 December 2017